Re
Thi
belo
tele

29.
1
C

0
22.
15.

=4 S
25 S

=6 NO

THE GIANT PANDA

Melissa Kim

Illustrated by
Shirley Felts

Hutchinson

London   Sydney   Auckland   Johannesburg

First published in 1995
1 3 5 7 9 10 8 6 4 2
© Text 1995 by Melissa Kim
© Illustrations 1995 by Shirley Felts
Copyright in this format © 1995 Signpost Books Ltd
Melissa Kim and Shirley Felts have asserted their right under the Copyright, Designs
and Patents Act, 1988, to be identified as the author and illustrator of this work

First published in the United Kingdom in 1995 by
Hutchinson Children's Books
Random House UK Limited
20 Vauxhall Bridge Road,
London SW1V 2SA

Random House Australia (Pty) Limited
20 Alfred Street, Milsons Point, Sydney,
New South Wales 2061, Australia

Random House New Zealand Limited
18 Poland Street, Glenfield
Auckland 10, New Zealand

Random House South Africa (Pty) Limited
PO Box 337, Bergvlei, South Africa

Random House UK Limited Reg. No. 954009
Conceived, edited, designed, and produced by Signpost Books, Ltd.
25 Eden Drive, Headington, Oxford, England OX3 0AB

Editor: Dorothy Wood
Designer: Krystyna Hewitt

A CIP catalogue record for this book
is available from the British Library

ISBN 0 09 176763 6

Printed in Hong Kong

SAVE THE PANDA

A soft and cuddly toy you want to squeeze, a roly-poly ball of white fur with a black mask, arms, and legs—this is what we may think a giant panda is. This charming creature has become the world's most beloved rare animal and the symbol for all endangered wildlife.

But the giant panda is not a cuddly toy—it is a wild animal. It is important to know what the panda is really like, so that we can fully understand its story and the danger it faces.

In the whole world, there are only about 1,000 wild pandas left. Why? Because man has taken away their homes and their food. Giant pandas are in serious danger, but you can help keep these fascinating animals from becoming extinct.

If you care about animals in danger, you automatically become a Wildlifer. Wildlifers are people who share a common concern for animals and want to do something to make the world a better place for the giant panda and for all of us.

Meet the giant panda

What could be more exciting and special than to see a giant panda in its natural habitat? But this is a privilege that not many people have had. There are so few pandas left that only a very small number of scientists and explorers have ever seen one in its home, high in the mountains of China.

Once pandas roamed across all of central and eastern China and even northern Burma, Thailand, and Vietnam. In these places, people have found fossils of animals that appear to be pandas and that are at least two to three million years old. About 20,000 years ago, after the last ice age, the number of pandas started to fall, and they began to move into the mountains of central and northwestern China.

In the last 2,000 years, the panda population has fallen sharply. The panda's home has been turned into farmland, so there is less and less available food for the panda to eat, and fewer places where it can live safely.

It is only in the last 100 years that we in the West have even known about the panda. In 1869, a French missionary named Père Armand David (the man who discovered Père David's deer) travelled to China. There he saw panda skins for the first time. He was the first person to tell the Western world about what he called 'the white bear'. In the 1920's and 1930's, a handful of Western hunters travelled to China in search of the giant panda. In 1936, an American woman named Ruth Harkness brought a live baby panda from China to America — the first live panda to be seen in the West. The panda, named Su-Lin, became famous overnight.

Now we see drawings and photographs of the panda so often that it appears the panda can be found everywhere. This is not true. The panda is a shy animal. It prefers to spend its life alone, hiding behind leafy stands of bamboo.

China

Vietnam

Burma

Laos

Thailand

Is the giant panda a bear?

The giant panda looks like a large black-and-white version of a teddy bear. It is a mammal, so it has warm blood, suckles its young, and has hair on its body. But scientists are not sure if the panda is really a bear. It shares many traits with bears, but it shares other traits with the raccoon family.

There is another type of panda, called the *lesser panda* or *red panda*, which looks like a small cat-like version of the giant panda. The red panda also lives in China and eats bamboo. Although they have the same name, the giant panda and the red panda may not be related. To be related they would have to have the same ancestors and share the same genetic material.

Scientists cannot agree. Is the red panda a raccoon? Probably. Is the giant panda more like a raccoon or a bear? It shares more traits with bears, but it is difficult to say. One panda expert says that when people ask him these questions, he answers, 'The panda is a panda.'

ALL ABOUT THE RED PANDA	
Body length:	Average 46 cm long
Weight:	About 3–6 kg
Colour:	Rust red with a long ringed tail, white face and ears, black eye patches, and a black stomach and legs.
Food:	Bamboo leaves and shoots, fruits, berries, and small animals
Home:	China, Nepal, and Burma
Life span:	About 13 years at the most
Habits:	Sometimes lives in small groups; likes to climb trees

FACT FILE

Many animals look alike but are not related. Other animals don't look at all alike but are related. Look at these pairs of animals. Are they related? The answers are on page 32.

- Koala/Wombat

- Hippopotamus/ Rhinoceros

- Elephant/Hyrax (rabbit-like land mammal)

- Otter/Beaver

- Dolphin/Killer whale

- Turtle/Tortoise

- Duck-billed platypus/Spiny anteater

- Bat/Crow

- Porcupine/ Hedgehog

ALL ABOUT THE GIANT PANDA

Body length:	Average 152–183 cm long
Weight:	About 75–118 kg
Colour:	White with black legs, arms, shoulders, eye patches, and ears.
Food:	Bamboo leaves, shoots, and stems; will sometimes eat meat, other grasses, and fruits
Home:	China
Life span:	About 30 years at the most
Habits:	Lives alone, mostly on the ground

Where does the panda live?

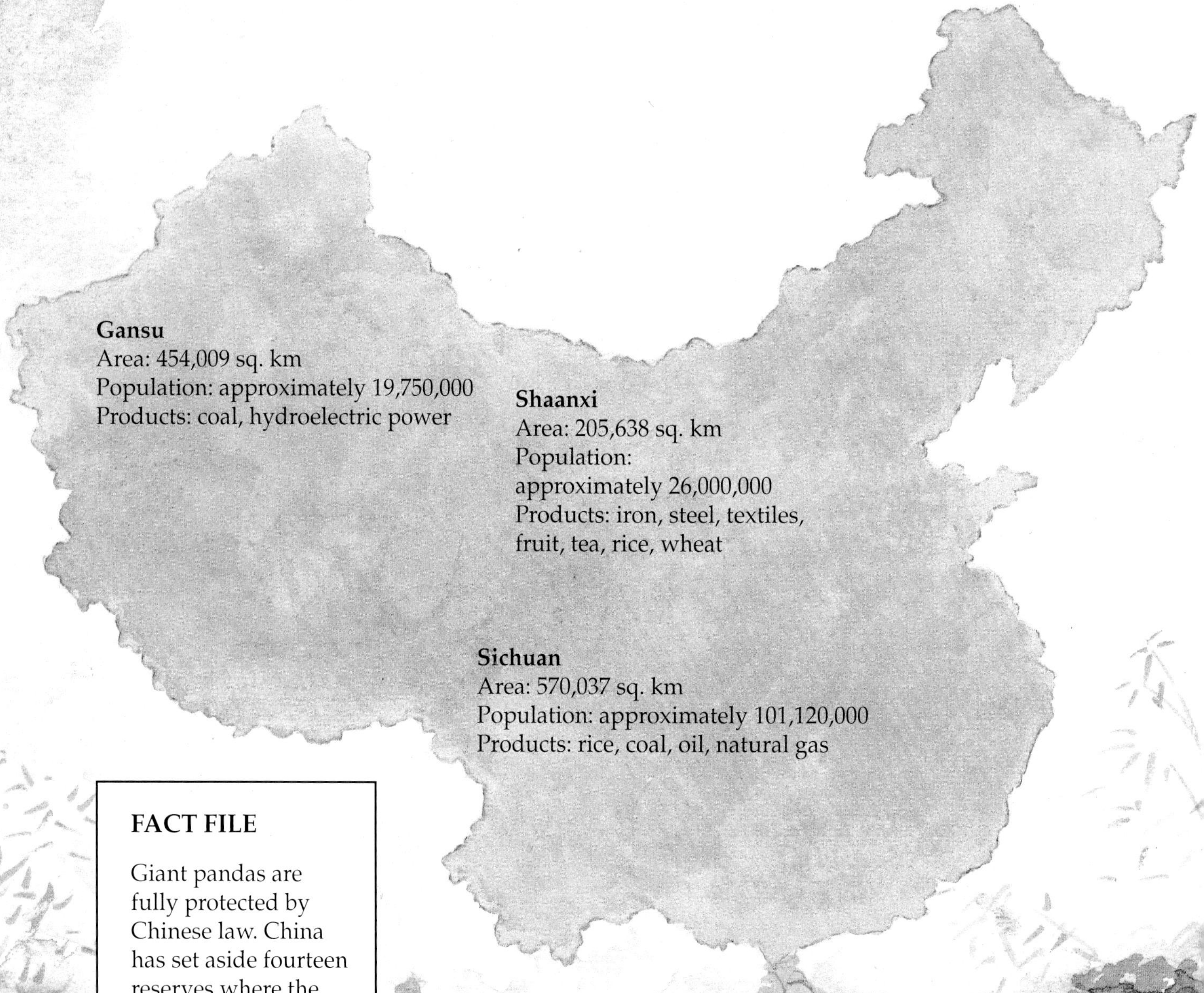

Gansu
Area: 454,009 sq. km
Population: approximately 19,750,000
Products: coal, hydroelectric power

Shaanxi
Area: 205,638 sq. km
Population:
approximately 26,000,000
Products: iron, steel, textiles,
fruit, tea, rice, wheat

Sichuan
Area: 570,037 sq. km
Population: approximately 101,120,000
Products: rice, coal, oil, natural gas

FACT FILE

Giant pandas are
fully protected by
Chinese law. China
has set aside fourteen
reserves where the
pandas should be
safe from harm and
where their homes
should be safe from
logging and farming.
There are eleven
reserves in Sichuan,
one in Gansu, and
two in Shaanxi.

Tucked into a remote pocket of China, between 800 and 1,300 giant pandas try to survive the cold winters and rainy summers of their mountain home. Most giant pandas live in the Chinese province of Sichuan. Others live in the neighbouring provinces of Gansu and Shaanxi.

Three mountain ranges stretch into these provinces. This is where the giant pandas live, between 1158 m and 3810 m above sea level. The only giant pandas in the wild live in six distinct areas within these three mountain chains. Within these six areas, there are approximately 24 isolated populations of pandas. That means that about 1,100 pandas are split into 24 groups. The groups are separated by clearings, roads, farms, and other obstacles. At least nine of these groups may have fewer than 50 pandas each, and some even fewer than 20.

The giant pandas prefer to live in the middle of a thick forest lush with bamboo. At lower altitudes, the bamboo stalks reach 183 cm high. The bamboo forest is tangled and thick, and it is hard for a human to work through. There may also be maple, birch, oak, or cherry trees. At higher altitudes, the bamboo is shorter, but thick rhododendron bushes and fir trees cover the ground. The rainfall is between 76 and 102 cm per year, and snow can fall from November to March. Mists, clouds, snow, and a thick forest canopy mean that it is always damp and wet, even if it isn't raining.

Characteristics of a giant panda

JAW
The giant panda has very strong cheek muscles and a powerful jaw. It would be hard to cut a thick bamboo stalk with an axe, but a panda can crush and chew it easily.

TEETH
The panda has two sets of teeth, baby teeth and adult teeth, just like humans. There are 42 teeth in a full set. They are thick, flat, and wide.

PAWS
The panda has one of the most unusual paws in the animal kingdom. On its two front paws, it has a 'pseudo thumb', or fake thumb. It's not actually a thumb, but a wrist bone that acts like a thumb. It helps the panda pick up and eat bamboo. The panda is one of only a few large animals (including humans) that can grasp objects well. It also has hair on the soles of its feet!

FUR

A giant panda's fur may look soft, but it is actually thick and coarse. It is about 4 cm long on the panda's back, 5–6 cm long on the shoulders, and up to 10 cm long on its belly. The dense fur protects the panda from the cold and prevents water from getting through to its skin, keeping the panda warm and dry.

SKIN

Underneath all this fur, the panda's skin is different colours! Beneath the black fur, the skin is black. Underneath the white fur, it is pink.

LEGS

The panda's legs are short, powerful, and very flexible. The panda walks with its feet turned in and rarely moves faster than a jog. A panda can use its foreleg to scratch the back of its neck or the top of its head. Or it may lift up a back leg and rest its head on it, using it as a pillow. The panda can twist and turn in all directions and even do somersaults!

Which way is this giant panda facing?

What's wrong with this set of footprints?

What's wrong with this set of footprints?

(Answers on page 32)

What do giant pandas eat?

A panda sits slumped against a small bush. All around it are tall stalks of bamboo. It reaches out, pulls on a stem, bites it off, and eats it like a piece of celery. When finished with one piece, it reaches out and pulls in another. All the panda needs lies within 91 cm of its grasp.

The panda's diet is 99% bamboo. On rare occasions it will eat fruit, other grasses, or meat if it can get it. That would be like eating spaghetti for 99 meals, having a hamburger once, and then going back to spaghetti.

The special diet has its good points and bad points. The panda probably became a bamboo eater because there was lots of bamboo around. No other animal eats all of the bamboo parts the way the panda does. It has special paws and teeth, just so it can eat bamboo more efficiently.

But the panda has the stomach of a carnivore—a meat eater. It has trouble eating and digesting plants. Bamboo is actually a very low-quality diet for the panda. It has to eat huge amounts of bamboo to get the nutrition it needs. It isn't able to store up enough fat to hibernate through the cold weather the way bears do.

FACT FILE

A giant panda may spend up to 16 hours a day eating. On average it eats 11–14 kg of bamboo a day. That means a panda will eat 4,536 kg of bamboo in a year. A panda may eat as much as half its body weight in bamboo shoots in only one day.

Divide your body weight in half. How many 113 g hamburgers would you have to eat to make up half your body weight?

FACT FILE

The panda's 'pseudo thumb' allows it to eat steadily and quickly. Once the panda has bitten off a bamboo stem, it holds it in a hairless groove between the pad of the first 'finger' and the bone of the 'pseudo thumb'. In this groove, the panda can easily hold even very thin stems of bamboo.

FACT FILE

The 'pseudo thumb' allows pandas to do all sorts of things that bears, raccoons, and other animals without thumbs cannot do.

In humans the thumb is an important feature that separates them from most other animals. Think of all the things you wouldn't be able to do without a thumb.

Make a list of all the things you used your thumb for today. Did you use a fork or pick up a glass? Try taping your thumb to your index finger. How easy is it to do the things you normally do? Try spending a day without using your thumb.

What is bamboo?

SHOOTS

In the spring, a new shoot pushes up out of the ground. Many animals, including pandas, love these fresh young shoots.

LEAVES
Pandas enjoy eating the leaves of bamboo. They are tough, so not many other animals eat them.

Bamboo is a type of grass that has woody stems and branches. There are more than 1,000 bamboo species, varying widely in appearance. Some species are short and thin, whilst others can grow as high as trees.

Giant pandas eat about twenty types of bamboo. In most of the places where pandas live there are four or five different types of bamboo growing. Bamboo thrives in the wet mountain climate. It's the only native plant that stays green all year long, even in the snow.

STALKS OR STEMS
As the shoot matures, it develops a tough woody stalk. Most animals don't or can't eat this part of the plant. The panda strips away the hard outer covering with its teeth and eats the soft fleshy part inside.

How does bamboo grow?

Bamboo plants reproduce in two ways. They have a system of *rhizomes*, parts of the plant that are like roots. These rhizomes sprout and poke through the surface of the ground each spring in the form of shoots.

Bamboo plants also produce flowers which have seeds. The seeds are spread by wind or animals. When the old plants die, new plants start to grow where the seeds have fallen. Unfortunately, all the old plants of a species die at the same time. This means that until the seeds grow into new plants, there will be serious feeding problems for pandas who depend on a particular type of bamboo, resulting in hunger and sometimes death. Usually pandas can switch to other kinds of bamboo, but often there is simply not enough food. The pandas' dependence on bamboo contributes to their shrinking population.

Strangely enough, there is a different length of time between flowerings for each kind of bamboo. Some flower and die as often as every 11 years, while others do so every 60 years. No one knows exactly how or why this happens.

How do pandas live?

A giant panda lumbers through the bamboo, stopping now and then to eat or to sniff a tree or a print in the earth. Then it stops. It senses another panda nearby, on another path in the forest. But it doesn't call out or walk to greet the other panda. Instead, it heads off in the opposite direction, so that their paths won't cross. The panda lives alone most of its life. It spends time with other pandas only when it is mating, or when it is a baby being cared for by its mother. It doesn't seem to need company. And yet, it leaves markings on trees and bushes to tell other pandas where it is. To do this, it has a special gland under its tail. It rubs against the trees and leaves a unique scent that other pandas smell and 'read' like a signpost.

Male and female pandas contact one another in the spring, when the time has come to mate. They have at least a dozen different calls and sounds they make at this time, ranging from barks and yelps to bleats, groans, yips, and hoots.

PANDA DAYBOOK

In the summer, pandas are active for 13–14 hours a day. In spring and winter, they are active for 14–16 hours, gathering and eating all the food they need to survive. They appear to have two long periods of rest a day, one just after sunrise, and one just after sunset when they will sleep for two, four, or even six hours.

FACT FILE

Pandas in zoos are famous for being playful. They seem to love turning somersaults and swinging in rubber tyres. Pandas in the wild may play, but they have to use most of their energy to collect and eat food. They climb trees only if they have to. However, one scientist saw a giant panda slide down a snowy hill on its stomach, and then do it again, for no good reason. Maybe it was fun!

A panda's year has three seasons:

SPRING

Bamboo shoots appear and the panda goes where the shoots are. Often the panda will come down from its high mountain home to eat the shoots of the *umbrella* bamboo. Springtime is also the mating season.

SUMMER AND AUTUMN

Monsoon rains come to parts of the panda's homeland. The bamboo plants are heavy with leaves, and the panda doesn't need to go far for food. It spends more time resting in the summer. Babies are born in August or September. The panda's *gestation period* (the time it takes for a baby to grow inside its mother) averages 140 days.

WINTER

Only old bamboo stems are left. The shoots have hardened, and most of the leaves have died. The panda has to eat more to get the energy it needs. Snow covers the ground, but the panda's fur keeps it warm. A panda stores up as much fat as it can to help it keep warm.

A giant panda is born

To get an idea of how light a panda baby is at birth, use some kitchen or postal scales to weigh objects such as books or food until you find something that's 100g.

A scientist tiptoes quietly and cautiously under branches, creeping toward the big fir tree where the giant panda has made her den. He peers in at the panda. Under the panda's large furry arm, the scientist can see a tiny pink fuzzy creature. It is small enough to fit into a human hand. It whimpers a little and the mother covers it with her paw, hiding it from view. The scientist is one of the few lucky people who have seen a baby panda in the wild. In August or September, pregnant pandas begin to look for large fir trees or caves where they can create a cosy den. A few days later they give birth to one or two cubs.

A baby panda is probably the most helpless and needy baby in the world. It weighs only 71–142 g, has no hair, and can't open its eyes. It is only about 15 cm long. The mother has to feed it, keep it warm, and protect it at all times. For months she never lets go of the tiny cub. If a panda has two cubs, probably only one will survive, as the mother simply cannot give enough care to both. After about 45 days, the cub will open its eyes and take its first look at the world. About a month later, it may crawl or take its first step. When it is five months old, it will be walking and tasting bamboo for the first time. It will already weigh about 10kg. At seven months, the cub can run, climb trees, and eat bamboo. But a panda cub may stay with its mother for up to two-and-a-half years.

It takes a lot of time and energy to raise a panda cub. Many die young. A female panda has a cub only once every 3–5 years. One panda would be lucky to raise five cubs in her lifetime. This is one of the reasons the panda population stays so small.

60kg

approximate weight*:

at birth: 112 g
1 month: 1 kg
2 months: 3 kg
3 months: 5 kg
6 months: 10 kg
9 months: 20 kg
12 months: 35–45 kg
*weights based on pandas in captivity

50kg

40kg

30kg

20kg

10kg

0

1 2 3   6   9   12
Months

Pandagraph

Baby pandas are tiny at birth, but they grow
very fast. On a piece of graph paper, see if you
can plot a similar line for human babies. Do you
know how much you weighed at birth? How
heavy were you at 12 months? How would a line
for humans compare to this line?

19

What threatens the panda?

Why are there so few pandas left in the wild? Sadly, humans are to blame. Even now it may be too late to save these shy and lovable animals. Pandas have suffered two major threats to their existence. One, poaching, is a serious and immediate problem. The other, the loss of land, is a long-term problem which pandas have endured for years and will continue to suffer from unless drastic action is taken immediately.

Poaching

Giant pandas have been hunted throughout history. Their pelt, or fur, has been prized and was thought to bring good luck. Even today, although pandas are protected by law, poachers still trap them and sell their pelts in Hong Kong, Taiwan, and Japan. One pelt may sell for as much as £7,000. If caught, poachers may face life in prison or even death. But according to one poacher, 'It's worth the risk.' The law is difficult to enforce, and poachers can trap pandas in the forests and never be seen.

Some pandas are accidentally caught in traps meant for deer, but others are intentionally hunted, caught in snares, or shot. Some pandas are even poisoned or bombed.

Loss of land

The other, long-term, threat to the panda is the loss of its home. China has a huge and growing population which needs land to live on and to farm. Between 1950 and 1980 millions of trees in China were felled to make room for people, farms, and smelting plants (factories to melt and process iron and steel). The area of China's land covered by forests decreased by 30 percent.

FACT FILE

There are fourteen panda reserves in China where the panda's home is safe. Plans and proposals for fourteen more are being considered. No logging is permitted on the reserves, but the people who have always lived there still farm and clear the land. Can people be asked to leave their homes or to change their lives to save a panda?

Today only 13 percent of China is covered by forest. In the three provinces where the pandas live, bamboo forests cover only between 10 and 36 percent of the land.

The giant pandas have been forced on to higher and higher ground and have broken up into even smaller groups. Scientists worry that the pandas may not be able to produce healthy cubs. Without large, old trees, a panda mother has a difficult time finding a good place to make a den and bring up her cubs. And without the forest canopy to create moist, cool soil and air, the bamboo doesn't grow well. So pandas are losing both their homes and their food.

The loss of forest land means disaster, not just for the giant pandas, but also for the people and environment of China. Without trees the soil cannot hold water when it rains, which leads to floods in the rainy season and drought in the dry season. The land erodes, or wears away, and nothing can grow.

Can scientists help the panda?

Many people have given their time and money to help the giant panda. Chinese researchers and a few Western scientists are studying panda behaviour, bamboo, and the entire forest habitat in the panda reserves in China. Their findings help us understand how the panda lives, and how we may find ways to protect it.

Captive breeding

Some scientists study pandas in zoos or research centres. They try to encourage the pandas to mate, either naturally or with artificial methods. This is called captive breeding. Some say that pandas born in captivity could then be released back into the wild to help increase the wild population. In fact, this has never happened, and captive breeding programmes have not been very successful.

Pandas in zoos

In 1936, when the Western world had its first glimpse of giant pandas, zoos were eager to buy and display them. But the desire for pandas was so strong, and the panda was so rare even then, that by 1939 China had put a ban on capturing pandas. Since that time, only about a dozen pandas have been sent to Western zoos. Today there are about 17 pandas in zoos outside China and about 90 captive pandas in China itself.

Pandas now come to the West only for visits, on loan to zoos for short periods of time. But not everyone thinks the practice of lending pandas is a good thing. Many people feel that pandas should not be taken out of the wild to be put into research centres or zoos. They also believe that those pandas already in research centres in China should not be shipped out of the country. In fact, both the Worldwide Fund for Nature and the association that oversees all American zoos have asked zoos not to 'rent' pandas. One fear is that pandas will be taken out of the wild and rented to zoos simply to raise money. With such a small number of pandas in the wild, this practice would be a disaster.

What do you think about zoos?

Do zoos help people learn about animals, or are they cruel prisons where animals are put on display for our entertainment? Answer the following questions to see how you feel about zoos. Make a note of your answers to each question and see how you scored on page 32.

1. The best kind of zoo…
a) gives an animal a home similar to its natural environment.
b) employs people who will keep the animals clean and well-fed.
c) has small cages so that it is easy to see the animals.

2. I like zoos because…
a) scientists can learn more about the animals and how to help them.
b) it's exciting to see animals from other countries.
c) animals are fun to watch.

3) I don't like zoos because…
a) animals shouldn't be taken out of their homelands.
b) animals shouldn't be in cages.
c) zoos are too expensive.

4) I think that animals are important because…
a) it's their world as much as it is ours.
b) we can learn things about ourselves from them.
c) we can use them for food, as pets, or to perform tasks.

5) The best way to learn about animals is…
a) to see them in their homeland (although this is often not possible).
b) to read books or to watch TV shows and films.
c) to see them in zoos or circuses.

6) If my local zoo were going to rent a panda, I would…
a) write and tell them not to do it.
b) ask them to only rent a panda that is too old to mate.
c) start saving money to buy my ticket.

Famous pandas

SU-LIN

In December 1936, the American Ruth Harkness went to China and became the first person every to bring a live giant panda cub out of the country. The cub was named Su-Lin, and its photo was on the front page of every newspaper in the world. The cub travelled to California and New York, and finally to the Brookfield Zoo in Chicago, Illinois, where it lived for more than a year. Su-Lin died in April 1938 of pneumonia.

MING

In 1938, the explorer, hunter, and collector Floyd Tangier Smith took five pandas to London. One died, one was bought by a German dealer, and two adults and a baby named Ming were left in London. Ming became as big a star in England as Su-Lin was in America. She boosted spirits during the war and was the mascot of many troops. She died in 1944.

CHI-CHI

Chi-Chi was caught in the wild in 1957 and taken to Beijing Zoo. She was destined for Chicago, but because of unfriendly relations between the USA and China, she was refused entry under the Trading with the Enemy Act. Chi-Chi then went to London Zoo. In 1964, it was suggested she be mated with Moscow Zoo's An An. Despite trips to and fro, they never succeeded in mating. Chi-Chi died in 1972.

LING LING AND HSING HSING

In 1972, the then President of the USA, Richard Nixon, travelled to China. As a gesture of friendship, China gave the USA two pandas, a two-year-old female named Ling Ling, and an eighteen-month-old male named Hsing Hsing. The pair became media stars overnight. Although Ling Ling had five cubs, all of them died soon after birth. The nation mourned when Ling Ling died of heart failure in 1993.

YING YING

In 1975, a female panda named Ying Ying and a male panda named Pe Pe were given to Chapultepec Zoo in Mexico City. In 1980, Ying Ying gave birth to a female cub, Tohui, which is still alive today. Tohui was the first panda to be born and raised outside of China. Ying Ying had two more cubs. She died in 1989, a year too soon to see her daughter, Tohui, produce her own cub in July 1990.

CHIA CHIA

In 1974, a pair of giant pandas were presented to British Prime Minister Edward Heath by the Chinese government. The female was never healthy and soon died. The male, named Chia Chia, travelled to many countries. In 1988, he visited Cincinnati, Ohio, for three months before going to Mexico to mate with Tohui at the Chapultepec Zoo. He briefly returned to Britain and, in 1991, returned to Mexico, where he later died.

FACT FILE
Many pandas are given double names. If you call someone by a double name like Ling Ling or Chia Chia, it is a sign of affection.

What can be done to help?

Many large environmental groups are working to save the giant panda. But so few pandas survive in China that action needs to be taken quickly, before it's too late. Surely one of the world's most beloved animals can be helped. There are several suggested plans for the panda's survival.

✳ NEW RESERVES

There are proposals for fourteen new reserves in which the land where pandas live will be protected.

✳ NEW BAMBOO

Many areas of the panda's home have been stripped of both trees and bamboo, so one way to help would be to replant these areas. However, any replanting needs to be carefully managed so that the right types of trees and bamboo are planted at the right times.

✸ NEW PATHS

Giant pandas live in isolated groups. It is difficult for them to travel to new areas. There is now an experimental plan to create corridors or paths planted with bamboo or trees and cleared of any barriers between the groups of pandas. That way, pandas might be able to seek new mates, search for new homes, or expand their home territories.

✸ NEW IDEAS

An important part of any plan for the pandas is the involvement of local people who have lived in these parts of China for years and do not understand why others want to save the pandas or the bamboo forests. They cut down trees and bamboo to create farmland. Scientists want to show them how the loss of bamboo and trees is bad both for the people and the panda's environment. Without education, any changes would be only temporary.

✸ NO POACHING

The killing of pandas must end. Local people must be stopped from trapping deer and, sometimes by chance, pandas. The poachers who kill pandas must be stopped. Right now there are not enough patrols to enforce the anti-poaching laws. With more money and more people, perhaps there could be more patrols and fewer poachers!

What can I do to help?

One day, a very long time ago, a Chinese girl came upon a leopard and panda fighting. The girl was afraid the panda was going to be killed. She grabbed the leopard and pulled it away from the panda. The panda escaped, but the leopard turned on the girl and killed her instead.

When the panda learned that the girl had died to save his life, he was very sad. He called all the pandas of the world together for the girl's funeral. They all wore black armbands. The pandas were so sad, they began to cry. As they rubbed their eyes with their black armbands, their eyes turned black. Hugging each other with grief, their bodies became covered in black patches. They covered their ears to muffle the sounds of crying, and their ears turned black.

This is the Chinese story of how the panda changed from a white 'bear' to the black-and-white 'bear' we know today. If you saw a panda being hurt, you might want to rush to pull the enemy away as the young girl did, but that could be dangerous. Here are some safer ways you can help save the giant panda.

Support wildlife conservation groups. You can write letters of support or raise money for them. You can buy books and products from companies that donate part of their profits to wildlife groups. These groups need to know which of their projects are the most important. If you tell them you think the panda is important, that helps them decide where to spend their money.

Educate others. Tell other people what you have learned. You could organize a 'Giant Panda Day' in support of the panda as a way to spread information. The more people know, the more they can help.

Go to the zoo. Research your local zoo. Does it treat the animals well? Does it import animals from other countries? Tell the zoo that you don't want them to rent pandas.

Any action you take to help endangered animals shows that you care about the world you live in. And that makes you a true Wildlifer.

Addresses

Worldwide Fund for Nature
Panda House
Weyside Park
Godalming, Surrey
GU7 1XR
ENGLAND

The Young Peoples' Trust for
Endangered Species
8 Leapale Road
Guildford, Surrey
GU1 4JX
ENGLAND

Panda a Go-Go

This is a game for two players. Each player has eight pieces (these pieces can be any flat small objects that fit into a square on the grid). They can be coins and buttons, or buttons and stones... just make sure each player has something different.

The object of the game is to surround *two* of your opponent's pieces so that they can't move. You try to surround your opponent's pieces, while he/she tries to surround yours, so it's a game of strategy. Players can move their pieces one square at a time. The pieces can only be moved up, down or side-to-side. They cannot move diagonally. Beginning with the pieces lined up at one end of the board, **Player A** moves one piece one square. **Player B** then moves one piece one square. You will also need to avoid the obstacles already on the board. You can get trapped against an obstacle. The first player to surround two of his/her opponent's pieces wins.

The game is a bit like a panda being chased by hunters or poachers. The panda can only move slowly, and sooner or later it ends up surrounded by people who want to kill or capture it.

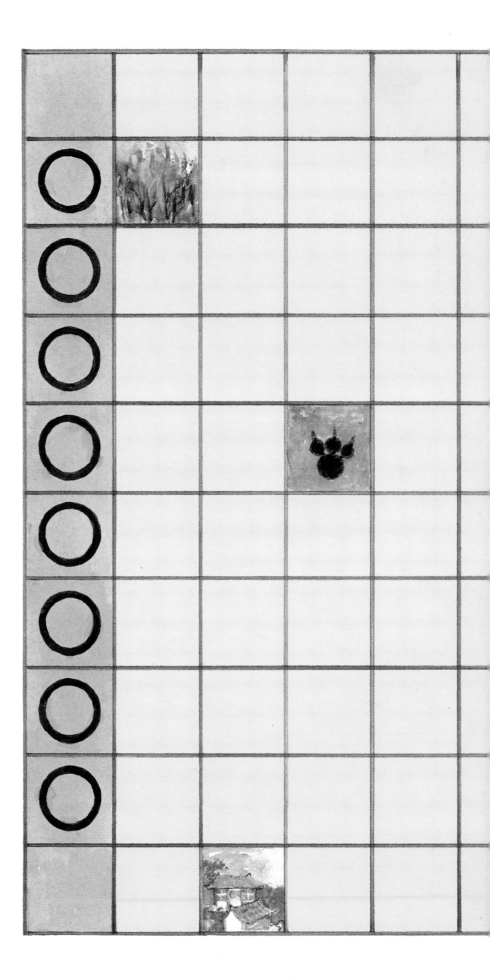

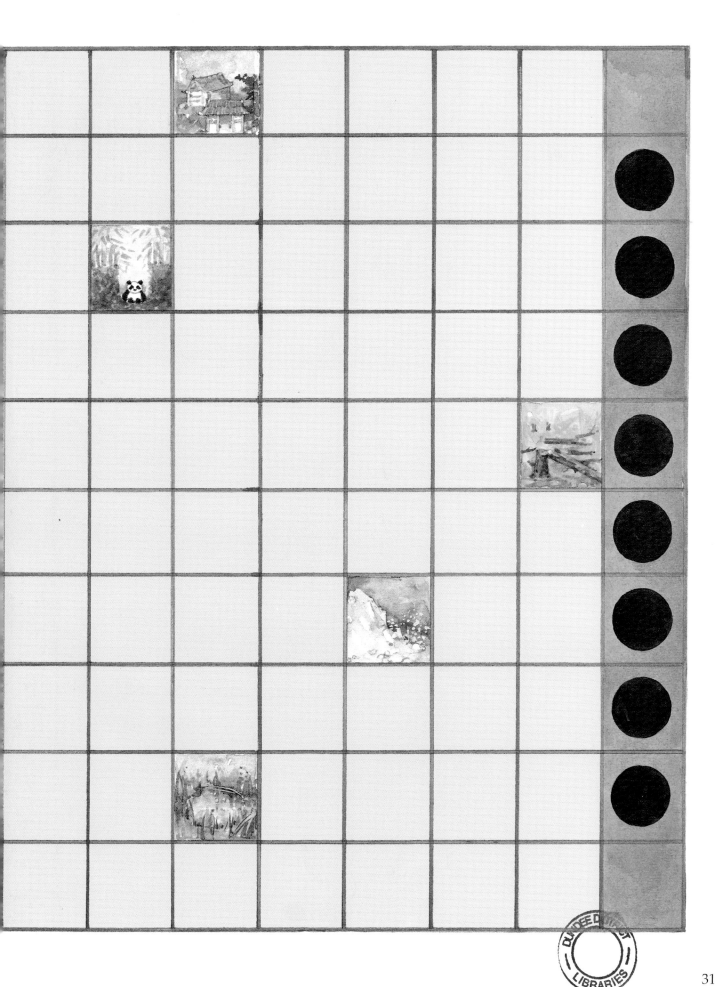

Index

Answers

Pages 6–7:
1) yes; 2) no; 3) yes; 4) no; 5) yes; 6) yes;
7) yes; 8) no; 9) no

Pages 10–11
a. The panda is facing to the right.
b. The giant panda's feet turn in. These prints are from an animal whose feet turn out.
c. The giant panda has six 'fingers' on its front paws and five 'toes' on its back feet.

Pages 22–23   Zoo Quiz

For every (a) score 10 points; (b) score 5 points; and (c) score 1 point.

41–60 points: You care a lot about protecting animals and nature. Good for you!

15–40 points: You like animals and nature, but you think that people are probably more important than animals. Ask yourself what the world would be like without animals.

0–15 points: Try seeing the world through the animals' eyes. Would *you* want to live in a zoo?